SERVING
ON A JURY

by Martha E. H. Rustad

PEBBLE
a capstone imprint

Pebble Explore is published by Pebble, an imprint of Capstone.
1710 Roe Crest Drive
North Mankato, Minnesota 56003
www.capstonepub.com

Library of Congress Cataloging-in-Publication Data is available on the Library of Congress website.
ISBN 978-1-9771-1398-6 (hardcover)
ISBN 978-1-9771-1822-6 (paperback)
ISBN 978-1-9771-1406-8 (ebook pdf)

Summary: Describes what juries are, who can be jurors, where they work, and more.

Photo Credits
AP Images, 25; iStockphoto: Chris Ryan, 18-19, dcdebe, 9, IPGGutenbergUKLtd, Cover, RichLegg, 5; NARA, 27; Newscom: File UPI Photo Service, 26, Jim Pickerell Stock Connection Worldwide, 15; Shutterstock: Alexkava, 7 (middle), america365, 7 (left, right),ESB Professional, 22-23, ggw, 21, Michelle Milano, 13, sirtravelalot, 10-11, 14; SuperStock: Hero Images, 16-17

Design Elements
Shutterstock: graphic stocker, Nadezhda Molkentin

Editorial Credits
Anna Butzer, editor; Cynthia Della-Rovere, designer;
Jo Miller, media researcher; Laura Manthe, production specialist

All internet sites appearing in back matter were available and accurate when this book was sent to press.

Printed and bound in China.
2489

Table of Contents

Words in **bold** are in the glossary.

What Is a Jury?

Have you ever needed help making a decision? When people need help making decisions about **laws** or rules, they go to **courts**. A **jury** helps the court make a decision.

A jury is group of 12 people. They listen to facts during a court case. Then they decide who is right.

A jury listens to the facts
presented in a court case.

Juries are part of the courts. Courts are in the United States **government**. The U.S. government has three branches, or parts.

The first part is the **legislative branch**. Lawmakers write laws and rules. The second part is the **executive branch**. This group makes sure people follow rules and laws. The third part is the **judicial branch**. **Judges** and courts make sure rules and laws are fair.

Federal Government

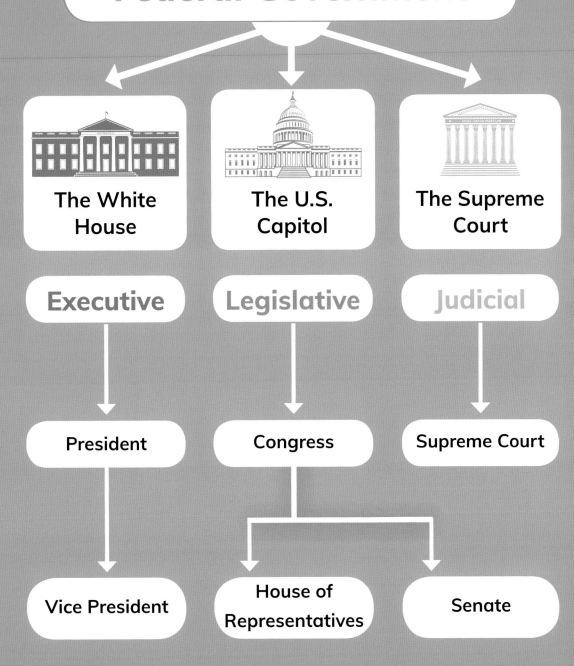

The White House — Executive — President — Vice President

The U.S. Capitol — Legislative — Congress — House of Representatives — Senate

The Supreme Court — Judicial — Supreme Court

Who Can Be a Juror?

Do you want to be a **juror**? There are a few rules about who can be one.

Jurors must be at least 18 years old. Only adults can be on a jury. They must be **citizens** of the United States. People born here are citizens. Some people from other countries choose to become U.S. citizens. A juror also must live in the county or state where a **trial** takes place.

All jurors are U.S. citizens.

Juries are made up of randomly chosen people. They are asked to come to jury duty.

Ordinary people are part of a jury. Someday you may be on one!

Sometimes people can't work on a jury. For example, a student might have to go to class. Someone might be sick or in the hospital. The judge decides if they can be excused. The rules are different in each state.

How are Juries Chosen?

Each state has its own rules for choosing jurors. Most courthouses get a list of people who can be on a jury. A computer randomly picks names off that list. These people get a letter asking them to go to the courthouse.

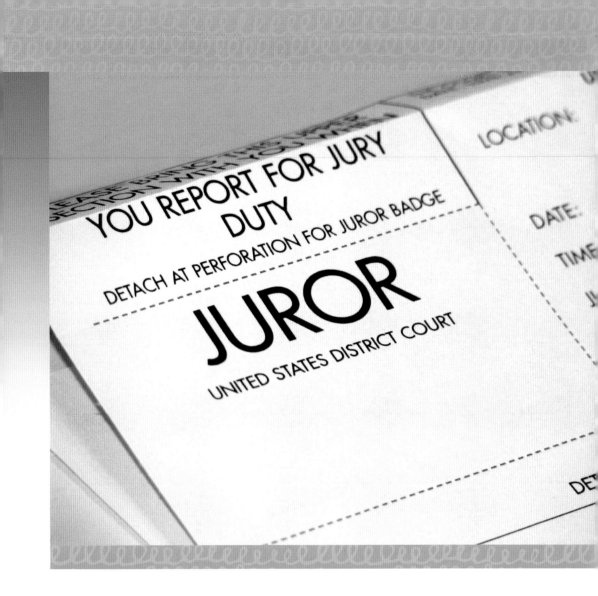

Judges ask these people questions.
Lawyers from both sides of a case ask
questions too. Jurors must be fair. They
need to listen to both sides.

The court finds juries for certain cases. Some court cases take only a few days. Others might last weeks. Sometimes a trial can take months. The jury must stay no matter how long the case lasts.

Jurors must take an **oath**. This is a promise to be fair. They promise to go to court and listen carefully.

Jurors must raise their right hands while taking an oath.

What Does a Jury Do?

Juries hear important cases. They listen to lawyers tell both sides of a case. People on a jury are quiet during a trial.

Judges give directions to juries. A judge also decides which facts or clues the jury can see or hear. Facts or clues in a case are called **evidence**.

Jurors listen to a judge and lawyers during a case.

In some cases, a judge decides who wins a case. Other times, a jury decides. A decision made in a court case is called a **verdict**.

Jurors don't always agree with each other.

Sometimes a jury can't agree on a case. The judge will ask them if they need more time to talk. A jury that can't agree is called a **hung jury**. The case ends without an answer.

Where Do Juries Work?

Juries meet in a courtroom. This is a room in a courthouse. This building usually is in the main city of a county or in a state capital city.

A jury sits on chairs in an area called the jury box. The judge sits at a desk called the bench. The bench is often raised up. Lawyers sit at tables in front of the judge. They stand up to talk to the judge or to the jury.

A courtroom has a jury box near the front of the room.

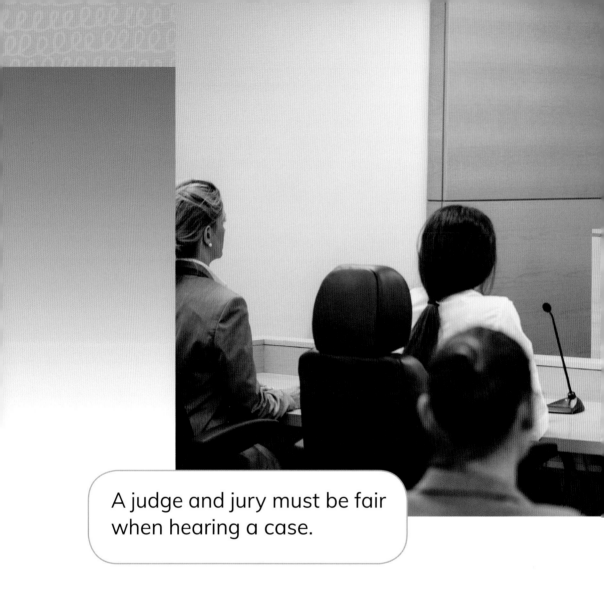

A judge and jury must be fair when hearing a case.

A judge can hold a jury. That means the jurors can't go home. They eat at the courthouse. They stay in a hotel. This does not happen often.

Jurors promise not to talk about the case when they leave the courtroom. They are not allowed to talk about the case with friends or family. They can't read or listen to news stories about the case. They must be fair.

Famous Court Cases

After a case ends, people can ask a higher court to listen to it. This is called an **appeal**. Some cases are heard many times. The Supreme Court is the highest court in the United States. It is the last stop for a court case.

Supreme Court justices, 1953

BROWN VERSUS THE BOARD OF EDUCATION

In 1954 the Supreme Court ruled that schools could not separate students based on skin color.

MIRANDA VERSUS ARIZONA

Ernesto Miranda was arrested for a crime in 1966. The police did not tell him his rights. He could stay silent. He could call a lawyer. The Supreme Court ruled that the police must tell people their rights.

Ernesto Miranda (right) and his lawyer

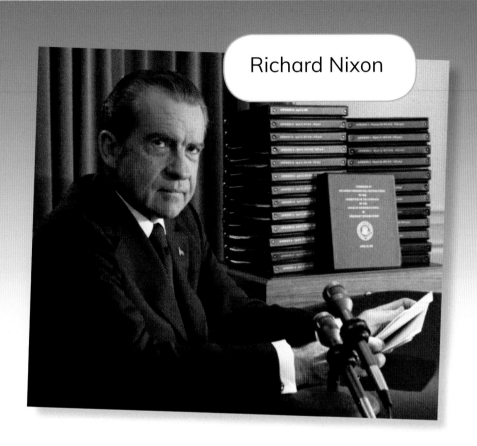

Richard Nixon

U.S. VERSUS NIXON

In 1974 important papers were stolen from Richard Nixon, a **candidate** for president. The Supreme Court ruled that even the president of the United States must follow the laws.

BETHEL SCHOOL DISTRICT #43 VERSUS FRASER

In 1987 a student made a speech at school. He used curse words. The school made him leave for three days. The case went to court. The Supreme Court ruled that students have to follow school rules.

TEXAS VERSUS JOHNSON

A man burned a U.S. flag at a protest. In 1989 the Supreme Court ruled that people could burn flags.

Fast Facts

Group: Jury

Role: Jurors listen to cases in court. They promise to be fair. They decide who wins the case.

How Jurors Are Chosen: The court gets a list of possible jurors. This comes from lists of voters or people with driver's licenses. A computer chooses people at random. Judges and lawyers decide who will be on the jury.

Pay: Varies by state, from $5 to $50 per day

Glossary

appeal (uh-PEEL)—to ask another court to review a case already decided by a lower court

candidate (KAN-di-date)—a person who runs for office, such as president

citizen (SI-tuh-zuhn)—a member of a country; a person becomes a citizen at birth or when they choose to become one as an adult

executive branch (ig-ZE-kyuh-tiv BRANCH)—one of the three parts of the U.S. government; this part makes sure people follow rules and laws

government (GUHV-urn-muhnt)—a way of making a country work

hung jury (HUHNG JU-ree)—a jury that cannot decide on a verdict

judge (JUHJ)—a person who is in charge of a court room and gives decisions in some cases

judicial branch (joo-DISH-uhl BRANCH)—one of the three parts of the U.S. government; courts and judges make sure rules and laws are fair

juror (JUR-ur)—a person who serves on a jury

jury (JU-ree)—a group of 12 people who listen to a court case and give a decision

lawyer (LAW-yur)—a person who studies the rules and laws of a country; they speak for people in court

legislative branch (LEJ-iss-lay-tiv BRANCH)—one of the three parts of the U.S. government; this part makes rules and laws for people to follow

oath (OHTH)—a serious promise

trial (TRYE-uhl)—the court process to decide if a charge or claim is true

verdict (VUR-dikt)—a final decision in a court case

Read More

Alexander, Vincent. *Serving on a Jury: Being an Active Citizen.* Minneapolis: Jump! Inc., 2019.

Heing, Bridey. *What Does a Juror Do?* New York: Enslow Publishing, LLC., 2018.

Manning, Jack. *Serving on a Jury.* North Mankato, MN: Capstone Press, 2015.

Internet Sites

Ducksters: Serving on a Jury
https://www.ducksters.com/history/us_government/serving_on_a_jury.php

Law for Kids: Goldilocks Trial
https://lawforkids.org/goldilocks

Index